Road Trip Alert:
Fun-tastic Activities
to Keep You
Wide Awake!

Lets Go!

RIDDLES AND QUIZZES

TO DISCOVER THE UNITED STATES OF

AMERICA

M&G Publishing

Visit us on the website, https://myamazingjournals.com,

Text copyright © 2023, by Ian Dix.

CONTENTS

RIDDLES

1. Riddle: I have a face on the dollar bill but I'm not a person. What am I?

2. Riddle: I'm a city known for skyscrapers, deep-dish pizza, and the Cubs. What city am I?

3. Riddle: I'm a statue that stands tall in New York Harbor, welcoming immigrants from afar. What am I?

4. Riddle: I'm a canyon in Arizona known for my vibrant colors and unique rock formations. What am I?

5. Riddle: I'm a musical genre born in the Southern United States, known for soulful tunes and a bit of the blues. What am I?

6. Riddle: I'm a state in the Pacific Northwest, famous for coffee, tech giants, and the Space Needle. What state am I?

7. Riddle: I'm a monument in South Dakota featuring the faces of four former presidents carved into the mountainside. What am I?

8. Riddle: I'm a river that flows along the border between Texas and Mexico. What am I?

9. Riddle: I'm a musical event that happens annually in the California desert, attracting music lovers from around the world. What am I?

10. Riddle: I'm a state that's home to the famous theme parks, Disneyland and Hollywood. What state am I?

11. Riddle: I'm a historic document that begins with the words "We the People." What am I?

12. Riddle: I'm a famous road that stretches from Chicago to Los Angeles, known for my role in American migration. What am I?

13. Riddle: I'm a holiday celebrated on the fourth Thursday in November, involving a feast with turkey and cranberry sauce. What am I?

14. Riddle: I'm a mountain range on the west coast, stretching from California to Canada. What am I?

15. Riddle: I'm a famous university in Massachusetts, known for my Ivy League education. What am I?

16. Riddle: I'm a city in Texas known for my cowboy culture, oil industry, and the Cowboys football team. What city am I?

17. Riddle: I'm a rock formation in Utah known for my unique red-orange color and towering spires. What am I?

18. Riddle: I'm a historical event that took place on July 20, 1969, involving a small step for man. What am I?

19. Riddle: I'm a body of water on the East Coast, famous for my sandy beaches and Atlantic City. What am I?

20. Riddle: I'm a city in the Midwest, often associated with the automobile industry and Motown music. What city am I?

21. Riddle: I'm a national park in Wyoming known for my geothermal features, including Old Faithful. What am I?

22. Riddle: I'm a historical trail that pioneers traveled in the 19th century to reach the West. What am I?

23. Riddle: I'm a state in the Southeast known for my peaches and the city of Atlanta. What state am I?

24. Riddle: I'm a major river in the United States, flowing from Minnesota to the Gulf of Mexico. What am I?

25. Riddle: I'm a national memorial in Washington, D.C., honoring the 16th President of the United States. What am I?

26. Riddle: I'm an island in New York Harbor, home to the Statue of Liberty. What am I?

27. Riddle: I'm a war fought in the 1860s over issues of slavery and states' rights. What am I?

28. Riddle: I'm a popular theme park in Florida, known for my Cinderella Castle and Space Mountain. What am I?

29. Riddle: I'm a state in the Midwest, known for my Great Lakes, automotive industry, and Motown music. What state am I?

30. Riddle: I'm a large desert in the southwestern United States, known for my saguaro cacti. What am I?

31. Riddle: I'm a famous avenue in New York City, known for my theaters and the annual New Year's Eve ball drop. What am I?

32. Riddle: I'm a state on the Gulf Coast, known for my jazz music, Mardi Gras celebrations, and the French Quarter. What state am I?

33. Riddle: I'm a national park in Alaska, known for my glaciers, wildlife, and vast wilderness. What am I?

34. Riddle: I'm a landmark in San Francisco, known for my orange color and suspension design. What am I?

35. Riddle: I'm a cultural and financial hub on the East Coast, known for Wall Street and the Statue of Liberty. What city am I?

36. Riddle: I'm a state in the Southwest, known for my deserts, the Grand Canyon, and the Colorado River. What state am I?

37. Riddle: I'm an annual event that involves watching the best commercials and a halftime show featuring top artists. What am I?

38. Riddle: I'm a historic site in Pennsylvania where the Declaration of Independence was signed. What am I?

39. Riddle: I'm a state on the West Coast, known for my tech industry, redwood forests, and the Golden Gate Bridge. What state am I?

40. Riddle: I'm a mountain range on the East Coast, known for my scenic beauty and the Appalachian Trail. What am I?

41. Riddle: I'm a state in the South, known for my country music, the Great Smoky Mountains, and Nashville. What state am I?

42. Riddle: I'm a famous battle site in Maryland, where a key battle of the Civil War took place. What am I?

43. Riddle: I'm a famous island prison in San Francisco Bay, known for housing Al Capone and other criminals. What am I?

44. Riddle: I'm a state in the Rocky Mountains, known for my ski resorts, national parks, and the Mile High City. What state am I?

45. Riddle: I'm a holiday celebrated on July 4th, involving fireworks, barbecues, and patriotic festivities. What am I?

46. Riddle: I'm a city in the South known for my country music, hot chicken, and the Grand Ole Opry. What city am I?

47. Riddle: I'm a body of water on the West Coast, known for my deep blue color and the Hollywood sign. What am I?

48. Riddle: I'm a state in the Midwest, known for my cornfields, the Field of Dreams, and the Hawkeye State. What state am I?

49. Riddle: I'm a mountain range in the eastern United States, known for my fall foliage and the Blue Ridge Parkway. What am I?

50. Riddle: I'm a city in Florida known for my theme parks, including the Magic Kingdom and Epcot. What city am I?

QUIZZES

1. Question: What is the capital city of the United States?

2. Question: Which state is known as the Sunshine State?

3. Question: What is the nickname for people from Texas?

4. Question: In which state can you find the Grand Canyon?

5. Question: What is the national bird of the United States?

6. Question: Which U.S. president is known for the Gettysburg Address?

7. Question: What are the three branches of the U.S. government?

8. Question: Which state is famous for its maple syrup?

9. Question: What is the longest river in the United States?

10. Question: Which desert is located in the southwestern United States?

11. Question: What do the 13 stripes on the U.S. flag represent?

12. Question: Which mountain range runs along the western edge of North America?

13. Question: Who was the first president of the United States?

14. Question: What is the largest state in the U.S. by land area?

15. Question: What famous document begins with "We the People"?

16. Question: Which state is known as the Land of 10,000 Lakes?

17. Question: In which city is the Statue of Liberty located?

18. Question: What is the national flower of the United States?

19. Question: Who wrote the Declaration of Independence?

20. Question: Which ocean is on the east coast of the United States?

21. Question: What is the largest city in California?

22. Question: Which state is known as the Last Frontier?

23. Question: In what year did Christopher Columbus first arrive in the Americas?

24. Question: What is the national mammal of the United States?

25. Question: Which river is often called the "Mighty Mississippi"?

26. Question: Who is known as the "Father of Our Country"?

27. Question: What is the nickname for people from New York?

28. Question: In which state is Mount Rushmore located?

29. Question: What is the official language of the United States?

30. Question: Which state is famous for its oranges?

31. Question: What is the highest mountain in North America?

32. Question: Who was the president during the Civil War?

33. Question: What is the national tree of the United States?

34. Question: Which state is known as the
Volunteer State?

35. Question: In which city is the White House
located?

36. Question: What is the official currency of
the United States?

37. Question: Which state is known for its
lobster?

38. Question: Who is on the $1 bill?

39. Question: Which state is known as the
Garden State?

40. Question: What is the nickname for
people from California?

41. Question: Which state is known as the
Show-Me State?

42. Question: What is the largest city in the
United States?

43. Question: In which state is the Everglades National Park?

44. Question: Who was the main author of the U.S. Constitution?

45. Question: What is the national fish of the United States?

46. Question: Which state is known as the Palmetto State?

47. Question: What is the official bird of the United States?

48. Question: In which state can you find Yellowstone National Park?

49. Question: Who is on the $5 bill?

50. Question: Which river is often associated with Mark Twain's stories?

51. Question: What is the nickname for people from Florida?

52. Question: In which state is the Alamo located?

53. Question: What is the national instrument of the United States?

54. Question: Which state is known as the Bluegrass State?

55. Question: Who is on the $10 bill?

56. Question: What is the official flower of the United States?

57. Question: In which state is the Great Smoky Mountains National Park?

58. Question: Which state is known as the Land of Enchantment?

59. Question: What is the national reptile of the United States?

60. Question: Who was the third president of the United States?

61. Question: Which state is known as the Treasure State?

62. Question: What is the largest lake in the United States by surface area?

63. Question: Who is on the $20 bill?

64. Question: In which state is the Kennedy Space Center located?

65. Question: What is the national insect of the United States?

66. Question: Which state is known as the Land of 1,000 Lakes?

67. Question: Who is on the $50 bill?

68. Question: In which state is the Redwood National and State Parks?

69. Question: What is the national gemstone of the United States?

70. Question: Which state is known as the Peach State?

71. Question: Who is on the $100 bill?

72. Question: In which state is Mount St. Helens located?

73. Question: What is the national river of the United States?

74. Question: Which state is known as the Keystone State?

75. Question: Who is on the $2 bill?

76. Question: In which state is the Great Salt Lake located?

77. Question: What is the national sport of the United States?

78. Question: Which state is known as the Land of 10,000 Islands?

79. Question: Who was the second president of the United States?

80. Question: In which state is the Gateway Arch located?

81. Question: What is the national dance of the United States?

82. Question: Which state is known as the Beaver State?

83. Question: Who was the president during World War II?

84. Question: In which state is the Badlands National Park located?

85. Question: What is the national tree of the United States?

86. Question: Which state is known as the Land of the Midnight Sun?

87. Question: Who is on the $10,000 bill?

88. Question: In which state is the Shenandoah National Park located?

89. Question: What is the national dessert of the United States?

90. Question: Which state is known as the Centennial State?

91. Question: Who is on the $500 bill?

92. Question: In which state is the Great Barrier Reef located?

93. Question: What is the national dog breed of the United States?

94. Question: Which state is known as the Old Dominion?

95. Question: Who was the president during the War of 1812?

96. Question: In which state is the Mount Rushmore National Memorial located?

97. Question: What is the national rock of the United States?

98. Question: Which state is known as the Land of 10,000 Lakes?

99. Question: Who is on the $50,000 bill?

100.	Question: In which state is the
Great Wall of China located?

SOLUTIONS

1. Solution: George Washington (on the one-dollar bill).

2. Solution: Chicago.

3. Solution: The Statue of Liberty.

4. Solution: The Grand Canyon.

5. Solution: Jazz.

6. Solution: Washington.

7. Solution: Mount Rushmore.

8. Solution: Rio Grande.

9. Solution: Coachella.

10. Solution: California.

11. Solution: The U.S. Constitution.

12. Solution: Route 66.

13. Solution: Thanksgiving.

14. Solution: The Sierra Nevada.

15. Solution: Harvard.

16. Solution: Dallas.

17. Solution: Bryce Canyon.

18. Solution: The moon landing.

19. Solution: The Atlantic Ocean.

20. Solution: Detroit.

21. Solution: Yellowstone.

22. Solution: The Oregon Trail.

23. Solution: Georgia.

24. Solution: The Mississippi River.

25. Solution: The Lincoln Memorial.

26. Solution: Liberty Island.

27. Solution: The Civil War.

28. Solution: Disney World.

29. Solution: Michigan.

30. Solution: The Sonoran Desert.

31. Solution: Broadway.

32. Solution: Louisiana.

33. Solution: Denali National Park.

34. Solution: The Golden Gate Bridge.

35. Solution: New York City.

36. Solution: Arizona.

37. Solution: The Super Bowl.

38. Solution: Independence Hall.

39. Solution: California.

40. Solution: The Appalachian Mountains.

41. Solution: Tennessee.

42. Solution: Antietam.

43. Solution: Alcatraz.

44. Solution: Colorado.

45. Solution: Independence Day.

46. Solution: Nashville.

47. Solution: The Pacific Ocean.

48. Solution: Iowa.

49. Solution: The Blue Ridge Mountains.

50. Solution: Orlando.

1. Answer: Washington, D.C.
2. Answer: Florida
3. Answer: Texans
4. Answer: Arizona
5. Answer: Bald Eagle
6. Answer: Abraham Lincoln
7. Answer: Executive, Legislative, and Judicial
8. Answer: Vermont
9. Answer: Missouri River
10. Answer: Sonoran Desert
11. Answer: The original 13 colonies
12. Answer: Rocky Mountains
13. Answer: George Washington
14. Answer: Alaska
15. Answer: The U.S. Constitution
16. Answer: Minnesota
17. Answer: New York City
18. Answer: Rose
19. Answer: Thomas Jefferson
20. Answer: Atlantic Ocean
21. Answer: Los Angeles
22. Answer: Alaska
23. Answer: 1492
24. Answer: Bison

25. Answer: Mississippi River
26. Answer: George Washington
27. Answer: New Yorkers
28. Answer: South Dakota
29. Answer: There is no official language.
30. Answer: Florida
31. Answer: Denali (Mount McKinley)
32. Answer: Abraham Lincoln
33. Answer: Oak
34. Answer: Tennessee
35. Answer: Washington, D.C.
36. Answer: U.S. Dollar
37. Answer: Maine
38. Answer: George Washington
39. Answer: New Jersey
40. Answer: Californians
41. Answer: Missouri
42. Answer: New York City
43. Answer: Florida
44. Answer: James Madison
45. Answer: American Goldfish
46. Answer: South Carolina
47. Answer: Bald Eagle
48. Answer: Wyoming
49. Answer: Abraham Lincoln
50. Answer: Mississippi River

51. Answer: Floridians
52. Answer: Texas
53. Answer: Banjo
54. Answer: Kentucky
55. Answer: Alexander Hamilton
56. Answer: Rose
57. Answer: Tennessee and North Carolina
58. Answer: New Mexico
59. Answer: Eastern Box Turtle
60. Answer: Thomas Jefferson
61. Answer: Montana
62. Answer: Lake Superior
63. Answer: Andrew Jackson
64. Answer: Florida
65. Answer: Monarch Butterfly
66. Answer: Minnesota
67. Answer: Ulysses S. Grant
68. Answer: California
69. Answer: Turquoise
70. Answer: Georgia
71. Answer: Benjamin Franklin
72. Helens located?
73. Answer: Washington
74. Answer: The Mississippi River
75. Answer: Pennsylvania
76. Answer: Thomas Jefferson
77. Answer: Utah

78. Answer: Baseball
79. Answer: Florida
80. Answer: John Adams
81. Answer: Missouri
82. Answer: Square Dance
83. Answer: Franklin D. Roosevelt
84. Answer: South Dakota
85. Answer: Oak
86. Answer: Alaska
87. Answer: Salmon P. Chase
88. Answer: Virginia
89. Answer: Apple Pie
90. Answer: Colorado
91. Answer: William McKinley
92. Answer: Australia (Note: This question is to mix things up!)
93. Answer: American Pit Bull Terrier
94. Answer: Virginia
95. Answer: James Madison
96. Answer: South Dakota
97. Answer: Granite
98. Answer: Minnesota (Note: Repeated question for review)
99. Answer: Woodrow Wilson
100. Answer: China (Note: Another mix-up question!)

THANK YOU!

M&G Publishing

Info.mandg.publishing@gmail.com

https://myamazinzjournals.com

www.ingramcontent.com/pod-product-compliance
Lightning Source LLC
Chambersburg PA
CBHW060850260726